The Berenstain Bears'
Holiday Cookbook
Cub-Friendly Cooking with an Adult

ZONDERKIDZ

The Berenstain Bears'® Holiday Cookbook
Copyright © 2016 by Berenstain Publishing, Inc.
Illustrations © 2016 by Berenstain Publishing, Inc.
Photography © 2016 by Ron Nickel Photography
(pgs 11, 13, 25, 27, 33, 37, 47, 49, 53, 55, 57, 59, 63, 65, 69, 77, 83, 91, 93, 95)

Requests for information should be addressed to:
Zonderkidz, 3900 *Sparks Dr. SE, Grand Rapids, Michigan 49546*

ISBN 978-0-310-75399-5

By Mike Berenstain
Based on the characters created by
Stan & Jan Berenstain

Editor: Mary Hassinger
Design: Cindy Davis
Printed in China

16 17 18 19 20 21 /LPC/ 9 8 7 6 5 4 3 2 1

Contents

We love because he first loved us.
—1 John 4:19

The Bear family love each other very much, so Valentine's Day is the perfect holiday for them! Mama Bear loves to show her cubs and Papa how much she cares for them by cooking up family favorite foods for a special lunch or dinner.

This year Sister asked Mama, "Can you help make Pink Party Popcorn for our class Valentine's party, please?"

And Papa and Brother requested Valentine's Day Pizzas! So the tree house kitchen would be a busy place.

Mama and Honey need to take a shopping trip to town. So they wrote a list of things they need for the special day's treats. Pepperoni for the pizza, more popcorn for the Sister's treat, and some big, juicy strawberries for a surprise were on the list, together with the usual honey, butter, bread, milk, and eggs.

"Chocolate too!" says Honey as she and Mama walk to the car.

Lord, we love you!
We are blessed
For food and family,
And all the rest!

Valentine's Day 🤍🤍

Pink Party Popcorn

What you need:

- 1 bag microwave popcorn
- ½ cup dried cranberries
- ½ cup semisweet milk chocolate chips
- 3 ounces white chocolate, broken into small pieces
- Red oil-based food coloring*

*Note: Do not use regular, water-based food coloring. It can ruin the consistency of your chocolate.

Directions

1. Pop the popcorn according to the directions on the bag. Place in a large bowl.

2. Add cranberries and chocolate chips to the bowl.

3. Put the white chocolate into a microwave-safe bowl. Microwave at medium heat for 30 seconds, then stir. Heat for another 30 seconds, repeating until the chocolate is melted.

4. Slowly add drops of oil-based food coloring to the chocolate while stirring until you have reached your desired pink color.

5. Drizzle pink chocolate over the popcorn mixture, and toss well to coat.

6. Spread out the popcorn mixture on a large baking tray. Allow to harden thoroughly, then store in an airtight container.

Yield: 3–4 servings

Red Bear-y Smoothie

What you need:

- 1 cup ice cubes*
- ¾ cup yogurt (try vanilla)
- 1 cup strawberries, rinsed with tops cut off
- 1 cup raspberries, rinsed
- 1 banana, peeled
- ½ cup orange juice

*Note: If you are using frozen fruit, ice can be skipped.

Directions

1. Add ingredients to your blender in the order listed. Place lid on the blender.

2. Blend until smooth, stopping the blender to stir occasionally if needed.

3. Pour into your glass and add a twisty straw for extra fun!

Yield: 1–2 servings

Tomato Soup with Grilled Cheese

What you need:

- 1 can favorite tomato soup
- 2 slices whole wheat bread
- Favorite cheese
- Butter or olive oil

Directions

1. Prepare the tomato soup according to the directions on the can.

2. While the soup is cooking, warm a pan on the stove at medium heat.

3. Use a heart-shaped cookie cutter to make a heart (or two) out of your slices of bread. You can also cut the hearts out by hand. Then butter the bread slices on one side or brush with olive oil.

4. Build your sandwich with the bread and as much cheese as you like. (You can cut the cheese into hearts too.)

5. Carefully set the sandwich in the warm pan, butter side up and down, and cook until the bottom side is lightly browned. Then flip the sandwich and cook until golden and the cheese is melting.

6. Dip your sandwich in your soup and enjoy!

Yield: 1–2 servings

Lovey-Dovey Banana Bread

What you need:

- 1-½ cups flour
- 1 cup sugar
- ½ teas. baking soda
- 1 teas. baking powder
- 2 eggs
- 2 ripe bananas
- ½ cup butter, melted
- ½ teas. almond extract
- ½ cup chopped pecans
- ½ cup chopped strawberries
- ½ cup semisweet or milk chocolate chips

Directions

1. Preheat oven to 350° F.

2. In a large bowl, mix together the flour, sugar, baking soda, and baking powder.

3. In a small bowl, mix together the eggs, bananas, butter, and almond extract.

4. Add the banana mixture to the flour mixture, then add pecans, strawberries, and chocolate chips.

5. Pour the mixture into a greased 9"x 5" loaf pan. Bake for 50 minutes or until a toothpick inserted near the center comes out clean.

Yield: 8–10 servings

Valentine's Day Pizza

What you need:

For the Crust
- 1 cup water, warmed to 110° F
- 1 package (.25 ounces) active dry yeast
- 1 teas. sugar
- 2-½ cups flour (bread flour works best)
- 2 tablespoons olive oil
- A pinch salt

Recommended Toppings
- Pizza sauce
- Mozzarella cheese
- Pepperoni
- Oregano

Directions

1. Preheat oven to 450° F.

2. Pour the warm water into a medium bowl. Add the yeast and sugar. Stir gently until dissolved, then let the mixture rest for 10 minutes.

3. Add flour, olive oil, and salt to the water mixture. Mix until the dough is smooth, then let the dough rest for 5 minutes.

4. Lightly flour your countertop or cooking surface. Once the dough is ready take it out of the bowl and shape it into a heart.

5. Place the dough heart on a pizza stone or lightly greased pizza pan/tray.

6. Add your toppings. If you are using the recommended toppings, first do a layer of sauce (leaving room for the crust and making sure the sauce isn't running over the edges), then add cheese and pepperoni. Finally, top with oregano to taste.

7. Bake the pizza for 15–20 minutes, or until the cheese and crust are golden brown.

8. Remove the pizza from the oven, allow to cool for a few minutes.

Yield: 4 servings

Yummy Chocolate Strawberries

What you need:

- 20–25 strawberries
- 6 ounces chocolate—try semisweet—broken into small pieces
- 3 ounces white chocolate for decorating, also broken into small pieces

Directions

1. Rinse strawberries under cool water, then pat dry with a cloth or paper towel.

2. Line a cookie tray with wax paper or parchment paper. Place the strawberries on the tray.

3. Put your semisweet chocolate into a microwave-safe bowl. Microwave at medium heat for 30 seconds, then stir. Heat for another 30 seconds, repeating until the chocolate is melted.

4. Repeat step 3 with the white chocolate.

5. Pick up a strawberry from the tray and dip into the semisweet chocolate. Make sure the strawberry is coated, and let the extra chocolate drip back into your bowl. Set the strawberry back on the tray. Repeat with the rest of your strawberries.

6. To decorate, dip a fork in the white chocolate and carefully drizzle over the strawberries.

7. Allow the chocolate to firm up for 30 minutes. You can leave the strawberries out on the counter or put them in the fridge/freezer if you want a cooler treat.

Yield: 20–25 strawberries

Sweetheart Chocolate Cake

What you need:

- ²/₃ cup butter, softened
- 1-²/₃ cups sugar
- 3 eggs
- 2 cups all-purpose flour
- ²/₃ cup baking cocoa
- 1-¼ teas. baking soda
- 1 teas. salt
- 1-½ cups milk
- 1 8–ounce package dark chocolate chips
- 1 can favorite frosting
- 1 pint strawberries, rinsed and dried

Directions

1. Preheat oven to 350° F.
2. In a small bowl, combine flour, cocoa, baking soda, and salt.
3. In a large bowl, add butter and sugar. Using a hand mixer, cream butter and sugar together.
4. Beat eggs into the sugar mixture one at a time.
5. Slowly add the flour mixture into the large bowl, alternating with the milk.
6. Add chocolate chips and mix until batter is smooth.
7. Pour batter into a greased 13x9 pan. Bake for 35–40 minutes or until a toothpick inserted in the center of the cake comes out clean.
8. While the cake cools, prepare the strawberries. Cut the strawberry in half lengthwise, then trim out a V where the stem is. Now you have strawberry hearts.
9. When the cake has cooled, frost and decorate with strawberry hearts.

Yield: 10–12 servings

He is risen!
—Mark 16:6

Easter! What a joyful time of year in the Bear's tree house and all over Bear Country! Dressed in their Sunday best and jumping with excitement to go to the Chapel in the Woods, the Bear cubs follow Mama and Papa out the door and head down the sunny dirt road with friends as they walk to Easter services.

"You are still coming to dinner, aren't you Farmer Ben?" Papa asks his friend as they catch up with Farmer and Mrs. Ben on the walk.

Mrs. Ben smiles at Mama Bear. "Wouldn't miss Mama's delicious ham dinner."

"The cubs helped get dinner ready this year. Brother tried something new—carrot chips! And Sister made the salad this morning," Mama says, proud of her cubs.

"'Tatoes, please," says Honey Bear.

"Yes, and we are having your favorite mashed potatoes too," Papa says åas he pushes Honey's stroller the rest of the way to church.

God's blessings at Easter,
To you and you and you.
Family and friends together—
A special blessing too.

Easter

Carrot Chips

What you need:

- 2 large carrots: rinsed, dried, and peeled
- ½ tablespoon olive oil
- Sea salt

Directions

1. Preheat oven to 350° F.

2. Carefully slice the carrots into rounds, about a quarter inch thick.

3. Place slices on a greased or lined baking sheet (or two), making sure they don't overlap. Toss with olive oil and salt to taste.

4. Bake for 12–18 minutes, turning once during baking.

5. Chips are done when the edges are golden brown.

6. Allow to cool 5 minutes.

Yield: 2 servings

Easter Bunny Shake

What you need:

- 1-½ cups mint chocolate chip ice cream
- ½ cup milk
- Whipped cream
- 1 small chocolate Easter bunny candy

Directions

1. Add the mint chocolate chip ice cream and milk to a blender. Put the blender lid on.

2. Blend ingredients until smooth.

3. Pour the shake into a glass and top with whipped cream.

4. Place the Easter bunny candy in the whipped cream.

Yield: 1 serving

Rabbit Food

What you need:

- 2 hearts romaine lettuce
- 1 seedless cucumber, sliced
- 1 cup red pepper slices
- ¾ cup sliced carrots
- ¾ cup cherry tomatoes
- Your favorite salad dressing

Directions

1. Arrange romaine leaves on a plate with their core ends touching in the center.

2. Layer cucumber slices over the romaine, then red peppers, then carrots.

3. Add a handful of cherry tomatoes to the center and edges of the salad.

4. Top with your favorite dressing, or use ranch for dipping.

Yield: 3–4 servings

Easter Ham Panini

What you need:

- 2 slices bread
- ½ tablespoon butter
- ¼ cup (2 ounces) fresh mozzarella, sliced
- ¼ cup leftover Easter ham, thinly sliced
- ¼ cup baby spinach or lettuce
- Half roma tomato, thinly sliced

Directions

1. Heat a panini maker. (If you don't have one, you can use a frying pan and put a smaller pan lid on top of the sandwich as the press.)

2. Spread butter on one side of each slice of bread.

3. On the unbuttered side of one slice, layer your ingredients like this: cheese, ham, spinach, tomato, cheese. Then add the other slice of bread.

4. Cook sandwich until the bread is golden and the cheese is gooey.

Yield: 1 serving

Honey Bear's Favorite Mashed Potatoes

What you need:

- 2-½ pounds yellow potatoes, peeled and cut into ½-inch cubes
- 2 tablespoons butter at room temperature
- 2 tablespoons cream cheese at room temperature
- ¼ cup warm milk
- 1-½ teas. sour cream
- Salt and ground black pepper to taste

Directions

1. Place potatoes into a large pot and cover with salted water; bring to boil. Reduce heat to medium-low and simmer until tender, about 20 minutes. Drain and transfer to a large bowl.

2. Mix butter and cream cheese into potatoes with an electric mixer or ricer until butter is nearly melted. Add milk and sour cream; beat until smooth. Season with salt and pepper.

Yield: 5 servings

Krispie Easter Eggs

What you need:

- 3 tablespoons butter
- 4 cups mini marshmallows
- 6 cups crisp rice cereal
- 12–15 plastic Easter eggs
- Small jelly beans or other Easter candies

Directions

1. Warm butter over low heat in a large saucepan.

2. Add marshmallows and stir until melted.

3. Remove the pan from heat and add the crisp rice, mixing together well.

4. Clean the plastic eggs and coat the insides with cooking spray.

5. Press the cereal mixture into the eggs. If you want to make a surprise egg with candy inside, press down into the halves of the eggs to make small hollows. Put candy in one half and then close the egg so the two halves stick together.

6. Allow eggs to cool, then decorate with your favorite Easter candy.

Yield: 12–15 eggs

Now the Lord is the spirit, and where the spirit of the Lord is, there is freedom.
—2 Corinthians 3:17

It's our country's birthday! The Fourth of July—and Bear Country celebrates in style.

Mama Bear decorates the tree house with red, white, and blue bunting and flags. Brother, Sister, and Honey decorate their bikes for the big parade down Main Street. And Papa Bear unpacks his old military uniform and puts it on to wear for the town parade. Everyone is excited for the summertime fun.

But best of all is the big Bear Country picnic in the park on Main Street. Everyone in Bear Country comes and everyone brings their favorite treats to share.

"I can't wait to have one of Missus Ursula's sloppy joes," says Papa as he pats his stomach.

It's hot and Mama is thirsty for the lemonade Gran and Gramps always bring.

Brother, Sister, and Honey are hoping for Papa's specialty—a big pot of baked beans! "You are making beans for today, aren't you, Papa?" asks Sister.

"Of course I am," Papa answers as he heads to the kitchen to get cooking.

To you Lord, we sing your praise
For family, friends, and holidays.
You give us all we have today
Freedom, food, fun, love—HOORAY!

Stars and Stripes Bites

What you need:

For Sweet Bites
- 3 cups red fruit (watermelon, raspberries, or strawberries*), rinsed and dried
- 3 cups yogurt- or white chocolate-covered pretzels
- 1 pint blueberries, rinsed and dried

*Note: If using strawberries, cut off tops

For Savory Bites
- 3 cups red pepper slices, rinsed and dried
- 3 cups cauliflower, rinsed and dried. You could also use white cheese cubes for this step.
- 2 cups blue tortilla chips

Directions

1. Line a baking sheet with wax or parchment paper.

2. Place a clear, square dish in the upper left hand corner. Add to the dish the blueberries for sweet bites or the tortilla chips for savory bites.

3. Starting at the top of the tray next to the dish, begin with a horizontal line of your red fruit or red pepper slices. Then add a line of white (pretzels or cauliflower/cheese). Repeat until you've reached the end of the tray.

4. Add a fruit or veggie dip on the side and serve.

Yield: 6–8 servings

Sparkling Raspberry Lemonade

What you need:

For the Raspberry Ice Cubes*
- 1 cup water
- ½ cup sugar
- 1 pint raspberries, rinsed

*Note: The night before you plan to have your lemonade, make the raspberry ice cubes.

For Sparkling Lemonade
- 1-½ cups sugar
- 1-½ cups water
- 1-½ cups lemon juice
- 2 cups sparkling water

Directions

Raspberry Ice Cubes:

1. Put water and sugar in a small saucepan. Bring to a boil over medium heat.

2. Add raspberries and simmer for 5 minutes, then remove from heat and allow to cool for 5 minutes.

3. Use a fork to mash the raspberries until all large pieces are gone. Cool for 5 more minutes.

4. Pour the mixture into ice cube trays and freeze overnight.

Sparkling Lemonade:

1. Put water and sugar in a small saucepan. Bring to a boil over medium heat, then simmer for 5 minutes.

2. Allow the water and sugar mixture to cool for 15 minutes, then pour into a large pitcher.

3. Pour in lemon juice and sparkling water and stir.

4. Add the raspberry ice cubes to the lemonade and sip away.

Yield: 4 servings

Firework Fruit Explosion

What you need:

- 1 cup grapes
- 1 orange, peeled and sectioned
- 2 cups strawberries, sliced
- 2 cups blueberries
- 2 cups cubed pineapple
- 3 bananas, sliced
- 3 kiwi, peeled and sliced
- $\frac{1}{3}$ cup lemon juice
- Sugar (optional)
- Miniature flag toothpicks

Directions

1. Rinse and pat dry all fruit, then cut according to the ingredients.

2. Put the fruit in a large bowl. Add lemon juice to keep fruit tasting and looking fresh.

3. Lightly sprinkle with sugar (white or brown) if desired, for extra sweetness.

4. Keep refrigerated until ready to serve. Add mini flags to the salad for a festive Fourth of July look.

Yield: 8–10 servings

Bear Country Pot of Beans

What you need:

- 4 slices bacon
- 1 small onion, diced
- 2–28 ounce cans baked beans
- 3 tablespoons molasses
- 2 tablespoons prepared yellow mustard
- ¼ teas. salt
- ½ cup diced tomatoes
- ½ cup brown sugar
- 1 tablespoon dry mustard
- ½ cup chopped cooked ham (optional)

Directions

1. Place the bacon and onion in a large, deep skillet. Cook over medium high heat until evenly brown. Drain and set aside.

2. Combine all the ingredients in a large crock pot and mix well, including the bacon and onion.

3. Heat thoroughly in the crock pot—about 3 hours on low.

Yield: 10 servings

Celebration Sloppy Joes

What you need:

- 1 pound lean ground beef
- ¼ cup chopped onion
- ¼ cup chopped green bell pepper
- ½ teas. garlic powder
- 1 teas. prepared yellow mustard
- ¾ cup catsup
- 3 teas. brown sugar
- Salt and ground black pepper to taste

Directions

1. In a medium skillet over medium heat, brown the ground beef, onion, and green pepper; drain well.

2. Stir in the garlic powder, mustard, catsup, and brown sugar; mix thoroughly.

3. Reduce heat and simmer for 30 minutes, stirring occasionally. Season with salt and pepper.

4. Serve on hamburger buns or rolls.

5. Add a flag toothpick for a patriotic look!

Yield: about 6 sandwiches

Red, White, and Blue Banana Split

What you need:

- 1 banana, peeled
- 4–5 strawberries, rinsed, dried, and tops cut off
- 12–15 blueberries, rinsed and dried
- Vanilla ice cream
- Chocolate syrup or hot fudge

Directions

1. Place the banana on a rimmed plate or oval-shaped bowl. Make a shallow cut longwise in the banana, then use a spoon to hollow out the top third to make room for the toppings.

2. Starting at one end of the banana, follow this pattern until the banana is full: 1 strawberry, 1 small scoop of vanilla ice cream, and then 3 or 4 blueberries in a clump.

3. Drizzle chocolate syrup or hot fudge as desired.

Yield: 1 serving

Freedom Trifle

What you need:

- 2–3.4-ounce packages vanilla pudding
- 1 premade angel food cake or pound cake
- 2 pints blueberries
- 2 pints strawberries
- Whipped cream for topping

Directions

1. Prepare pudding according to the directions on the package, then place in the refrigerator to chill.

2. Slice angel food cake or pound cake into 1-inch pieces.

3. Rinse and dry the fruit, then hull and slice the strawberries.

4. When the pudding has chilled, layer in this pattern in a trifle dish (or large glass bowl): cake, blueberries, pudding, strawberries. Repeat until you reach the top of the dish.

5. Keep in the fridge until ready to serve.

6. Serve topped with whipped cream.

Yield: 8–10 servings

The Lᴏʀᴅ will indeed give what is good, and our land will yield its harvest. Righteousness goes before him and prepares the way for his steps.
—Psalm 85:12–13

"There's a Fall Festival at the Bear Country School this weekend," says Brother, excitedly. "Can we all go, Mama?"

"I don't see why not. Tell us what is going on," Mama says.

So Brother and Sister showed Mama and Papa Bear the flyer. The school is celebrating good friends, sharing, and family togetherness. There will be games, a costume parade, a bake sale, and a dinner for the students and parents of the Bear Country School at the festival. Each family is asked to bring one or two of their favorite foods to share.

"Sounds like lots of fun to me too," says Papa. "I hope there's going to be candy and bobbing for apples!"

"Mama? Can we make trail mix to share?" asks Sister. "I'll help you."

Mama smiles. "Of course we can, Sister. And maybe a batch of chicken wings too."

"Mmmmm," Papa and Honey Bear say at the same time.

"There's going to be a sale too, to raise money to fill food baskets for the needy bears in the area. Can we make something for that, Mama?" adds Brother.

"Absolutely! Let's go look for a good recipe, Brother," answers Mama as she takes out her favorite cookbook.

Open hands and open hearts
And giving with good cheer,
Help those in need know just how much
They're cared for through the year.

Fall Festivities

Tricks and Treats Trail Mix

What you need:

- 2 cups Chex™ cereal
- 1 cup favorite nuts (peanuts, cashews, etc.)
- ½ cup small pretzels
- ½ cup raisins or other dried fruit
- ½ cup chocolate chips
- ¼ cup M&M's®
- ¼ cup candy corn

Directions

1. In a large bowl, combine all ingredients. Mix until evenly distributed.

2. Serve in small cups, little plastic pumpkins, or plastic sandwich bags.

Yield: 5–6 servings

Candy Corn Punch

Directions

1 Place one pineapple chunk in each section of an ice cube tray, fill the tray with orange juice, and freeze overnight.

2 Place several juice cubes in a cup.

3 Carefully pour orange soda over the cubes, about ¾ of the way full.

4 Add whipped cream and a candy corn piece to decorate.

5 Serve with a straw.

Yield: 1–2 servings

What you need:

- 1-12 ounce orange soda
- Orange juice
- Pineapple chunks, drained
- Whipped cream
- Candy corn

Creepy Crawly Pasta Salad

What you need:

- ½ cup each of three pasta types (try cavatappi, fusilli, rotini for a good creepy crawly mix)
- 8 slices crisply cooked bacon, chopped
- 2 cups shredded cheddar cheese
- 1 cup grape or cherry tomatoes, rinsed and dried
- 1 zucchini or small yellow squash, rinsed and dried
- Italian dressing (or dressing of your choice)
- Salt and pepper to taste

Directions

1. Cook pasta according to package directions, drain, and run under cold water to cool. Transfer pasta to a large bowl.

2. Add bacon, cheddar cheese, and tomatoes.

3. Slice the zucchini or squash into quarter-inch rounds. Carefully carve jack-o-lantern faces into some of the slices.

4. Add squash to the bowl.

5. Add dressing, salt, and pepper as desired.

Want to make this recipe even more fun? Try dying your pasta! Get as many large freezer bags as you want colors (if you want three different colors—like orange, green, and purple—get three bags). Put 1-½ tablespoons of water and 10-15 drops of food coloring in the bag(s). When the pasta has been cooked, drained, and rinsed with cold water, add it to the bag(s) of color. Mix the pasta around, then let it sit for a few minutes to soak up the color. Rinse once more under cold water.

Yield: 3–4 servings

Oven Roasted Corn on the Cob

What you need:

- 5 ears of corn, husks and silk removed
- ½ cup mayonnaise
- 1 cup parmesan cheese
- 1 tablespoon chili powder
- 1 teas. ground black pepper
- 2 tablespoon chopped parsley

Directions

1. Preheat oven to 400° F.

2. Cut 5 squares of foil, 1-½ times the size of the ears of corn and place each ear in the center of a square.

3. Mix the mayo, parmesan cheese, chili powder, pepper, and parsley in a small bowl until it forms a thick paste. Rub or brush about 2 tablespoons of the paste over each ear of corn. Wrap the foil around the corn, sealing tight. Arrange on a baking sheet.

4. Roast in the preheated oven for 10 minutes, turn each ear, and continue baking 10–15 minutes longer.

Yield: 5 servings

Papa's Paw-Lickin' Good Chicken Wings

What you need:

- ¾ cup all-purpose flour
- ½ teas. cayenne pepper
- ½ teas. garlic powder
- ½ teas. salt
- 20 chicken wings (Pat dry with a paper towel.)
- ½ cup melted butter
- ½ cup hot sauce or BBQ sauce

Directions

1. Line a baking sheet with aluminum foil and spray lightly with cooking spray. Put the flour, cayenne pepper, garlic powder, and salt in a re-sealable plastic bag, and shake to mix together. Add the chicken wings to the bag, seal, and shake until well-coated with the flour mixture. Place the wings on the baking sheet and refrigerate for at least 1 hour.

2. Preheat oven to 400° F.

3. Whisk together the melted butter and hot sauce in a small bowl. Dip each wing into the butter and place back on the baking sheet. Bake until the wings are no longer pink inside and are crispy on the outside, about 45 minutes. Turn the wings over about halfway through the baking so they cook evenly.

Yield: about 5 servings

60

Caramel Apple Nachos

What you need:

- 2 apples, rinsed and dried
- 15–20 caramels
- ½ teaspoon water
- Autumn-colored sprinkles

Directions

1 Core and slice the apples, then arrange on a plate.

2 Put the caramels and water in a microwave safe bowl. Microwave at medium heat for 30 seconds, then stir. Heat for another 30 seconds, repeating until the caramels are melted.

3 Allow caramel to cool for 1 minute, then pour over the apples.

4 Add sprinkles for an autumn look.

Yield: 3–4 servings

Wiggle and Jiggle Gelatin Bites

What you need:

- 2 3-ounce packages of JELL-O® (We recommend green, yellow, or orange for an autumn look.)
- 2-½ cups boiling water
- Themed cookie cutters (smaller sizes work better)
- 2 5-ounce packages of gummy worms

Directions

1. In a large bowl, combine the JELL-O and the boiling water. Stir 3–4 minutes.

2. Pour the mixture into a 13 x 9 inch pan. Put the pan in the fridge for 4–5 hours.

3. Fill your sink or a bathtub with warm water. Carefully dip the bottom of the pan into the water for 15–20 seconds to loosen the JELL-O.

4. Use your Halloween-themed cookie cutters to cut out festive shapes. Place the pieces on a large tray or bowl.

5. Add the gummy worms for more squirmy wormy fun.

Yield: 12–15 servings

Our God, we give you thanks. We praise your glorious name.
—I Chronicles 29:13

Thanksgiving is a special time of year for the Bear family. They spend lots of time together, but during the Thanksgiving holiday, the Bears include friends and family in many of their celebrations.

"When are we leaving for Grizzly Gramps and Gran's, Mama?" Sister asks while she watches Mama cutting vegetables. It's the day after Thanksgiving.

"Not for a while, Sister. I'm using some of the leftover turkey from yesterday's feast to make soup and I'm just getting started."

"Soup?" Papa walks into the tree house kitchen, looking for a snack. "Did I just hear you say you are making soup?"

Mama smiles. "Yes, Papa. It is for lunch today at Gramps and Gran's house. Remember, Missus Ursula and Farmer and Mrs. Ben will be there too."

"I hope there's some pumpkin pie left from yesterday. Gran makes the BEST!" Brother pipes up.

"We were blessed with so many pumpkins in this year's harvest I am sure Gran will be making lots of pumpkin pies all year long," Papa says.

"Thanks, God!" said Honey Bear, sneaking a carrot from Mama's pile of veggies.

Mama, Papa, Sister, Brother, little Honey too—
They all give thanks and pray
To God who gives us food and family,
Home and heart and night and day.

Thanksgiving

Gobbler Apple Muffins

What you need:

- 2 apples
- 1-½ cups all-purpose flour
- ¾ cup white sugar
- ½ teas. salt
- 2 teas. baking powder
- 1 teas. ground cinnamon
- ⅓ cup vegetable oil
- 1 egg
- ⅓ cup milk
- 12 sets of candy eyes
- 12 pieces of candy corn

Directions

1. Preheat oven to 400° F. Add 12 liners or lightly grease muffin tin cups.

2. Cut one of the apples in half. Peel and core the whole apple and one of the apple halves. Chop into small pieces.

3. Remove the core of the remaining half apple, but keep the skin on. Cut into matchsticks (about 1/8 inch wide pieces). Put these aside for decorating.

4. In a large mixing bowl, combine the flour, sugar, salt, baking powder, and cinnamon. Stir, then mix in oil, egg, and milk. Finally, add the apple pieces.

5. Pour batter into muffin cups, filling ⅔ full.

6. Bake for 20–25 minutes, or until a toothpick inserted into the muffin comes out clean.

7. After the muffins are done and have cooled for 5 minutes, add the candy eyes and candy corn "beak" to the center of the top of the muffin to make a turkey's face.

8. Insert the apple matchsticks in a semicircle around the outer edge of the muffin for turkey feathers.

Yield: 12 muffins

Hot Apple Cinnamon Cider

What you need:

- 8 cups (½ gallon) apple cider
- ⅓ cup maple syrup
- 1 teas. cinnamon
- 1 apple, rinsed and dried

Directions

1. Pour cider, maple syrup, and cinnamon into a large pot. Heat over medium heat for 5 minutes, stirring occasionally.

2. While the cider is heating, slice your apple into eighths or rounds. Cut a notch in the center of each slice.

3. When the cider is done, pour into mugs, then garnish with an apple slice.

Yield: 8 servings

Mama Bear's Turkey and Veggie Soup

What you need:

- 2 tablespoons butter
- 1 onion, chopped
- 1 stalk celery, chopped
- 2 large carrots, peeled and sliced
- 2 potatoes, peeled and cubed
- 3 tablespoons all-purpose flour
- 3 cups chicken stock
- ¼ teas. dried marjoram
- 2 cups cubed leftover Thanksgiving turkey
- 1 cup corn kernels
- 1 green bell pepper, diced

Directions

1. Melt the butter in a pan over medium heat. Add onion and cook until tender. Add the celery and carrots and cook until tender. Stir in the potatoes and flour. Add the chicken stock, marjoram, and turkey. Bring to a boil.

2. Reduce heat, cover the soup, and simmer for about 30 minutes.

3. Add the green pepper and corn and continue cooking for 10 minutes, until the peppers are tender.

4. Serve in mugs or bowls.

Yield: 4 servings

GOD BLESS OUR HOME

Cornbread with Honey Butter

What you need:

Honey Butter
- ½ cup (1 stick) butter at room temperature
- 2 tablespoons honey
- Dash of ground cinnamon

Cornbread
- ¼ cup (½ stick) butter
- 1 cup milk
- 2 large eggs
- 1-¼ cups cornmeal
- 1 cup flour
- ⅓ cup sugar
- 1 tablespoons baking powder
- ½ teas. salt

Directions

For the Honey Butter:

1. Cut butter into small pieces.

2. Place butter in a small bowl and beat at low speed with a hand mixer (or use a standing mixer).

3. Add the honey and cinnamon. Increase the mixing speed to medium and beat until well combined.

4. Place butter on parchment paper or plastic wrap. Form into a stick or round and refrigerate for several hours before using.

For the Cornbread:

1. Preheat oven to 400° F.

2. Put butter in a microwave safe bowl and microwave in 15-second increments until just melted.

3. In a small bowl, combine cornmeal, flour, sugar, baking powder, and salt.

4. In a large bowl, add butter, milk, and eggs. Beat with hand mixer.

5. Add the dry mixture to the large bowl and stir until just combined. Lumps are okay!

6. Pour into greased round pan.

7. Bake 20–25 minutes or until toothpick inserted in center comes out clean.

8. Serve with honey butter.

Yield: 8 servings

Stuffing with Cranberries

What you need:

- 1 cup chicken broth
- 1 cup chopped celery
- ½ cup chopped onion
- 10 slices whole wheat bread, toasted in the oven then cut into cubes
- ¼ cup chopped parsley
- 1 teas. dried tarragon
- ½ teas. paprika
- ⅛ teas. ground nutmeg
- ½ cup chopped fresh cranberries
- 1 cup chopped water chestnuts
- 1 cup chopped apple (leave skin on)

Directions

1. Heat oven to 350° F. Lightly coat a 2-quart baking dish with cooking spray.

2. In a large skillet, heat the chicken broth over medium heat. Add the celery and onion and saute until the vegetables are tender, about 5 minutes. Remove from heat.

3. In a large bowl, combine the bread cubes, parsley, tarragon, paprika, nutmeg, cranberries, water chestnuts, and apples. Add the celery and onion mixture and stir to mix evenly.

4. Place in the baking dish. Cover with aluminum foil and bake for 20 minutes. Uncover and bake an additional 10 minutes. Serve immediately.

Yield: 6 servings

Grizzly Gran's Famous Pumpkin Pie

What you need:

- 1 9-inch unbaked deep dish pie crust
- ¾ cup white sugar
- 1 teas. ground cinnamon
- ½ teas. salt
- ½ teas. ground ginger
- ¼ teas. ground cloves
- 2 eggs
- 1 15-oz. can pure pumpkin
- 1 12-oz. can evaporated milk

Directions

1. Preheat oven to 425° F.

2. Combine sugar, salt, cinnamon, ginger, and cloves in a small bowl. Beat eggs lightly in a large bowl. Stir in pumpkin and sugar/spice mix. Gradually add the evaporated milk. Pour into the pie shell.

3. Bake for 15 minutes at 425°. Reduce temperature to 325° F. Bake for 40–50 more minutes or until knife inserted near the center comes out clean. Cool on a wire rack for 2 hours. Serve immediately or refrigerate.

Yield: 16 servings

"May glory be given to God in the highest heaven! And may peace be given to those he is pleased with on earth!"
—Luke 2:14

The Christmas Pageant was over and the Bear family head back to the tree house through the crisp, cold night. The stars seem extra bright in the winter sky. And the snow crunches under their feet as they walk.

"How about some hot cocoa and sugar cookies when we get back home?" Mama asks her family.

"Do we have marshmallows?" "Can I use the snowbear mug, please?" "Mmmm, cocoa!" all the cubs answer at once.

Mama smiles. "I think we should set some cookies aside so we can bring a plate to Mizz McGrizz in the morning. She's had a cold and didn't finish her Christmas baking yet. What do you think, cubs?"

Sister agrees, "Yes, and I made a Christmas card for her. Can we bring that to Mizz McGrizz too?"

"God loves a cheerful giver," said Papa as the family walks across the tree house yard, admiring the soft glow of the Christmas lights on the fresh snow.

Christmas is filled with many things
From family, food, and songs to sing.
A special birthday on this date
Gives Bears cause to celebrate!

Christmas

Holiday Pinwheels

What you need:

- 1 medium red pepper
- 1 medium green pepper
- 2 8-ounce packages cream cheese, softened
- 1 packet (1 ounce) ranch dressing mix
- ½ cup shredded cheddar cheese
- ½ cup finely diced turkey or ham
- 6 flour tortillas

Directions

1. Rinse, dry, and dice the red and green peppers (removing seeds). Set aside.

2. In a small mixing bowl, add the ranch dressing mix to the softened cream cheese (you don't have to use the whole packet—just use to taste).

3. Spread the cream cheese mixture on one side of each tortilla.

4. Sprinkle the tortilla with peppers, cheese, and meat.

5. Roll up the tortillas and wrap tightly with aluminum foil or plastic wrap.

6. Store in the fridge for at least 2 hours and up to 12 hours. When you're ready to serve, take them out of the foil and slice into 1-inch pieces.

Yield: 10 servings (2 pinwheels per person)

Cozy Hot Cocoa

What you need:

- 2 cups milk
- 3 tablespoons unsweetened cocoa powder
- 2 tablespoons sugar
- ⅓ teas. vanilla extract
- Marshmallows (regular size or miniature)
- 2–3 candy canes

Directions

1. Add ½ cup milk to a small saucepan. Add the cocoa powder and sugar, and whisk together. Heat over medium heat until the sugar has dissolved.

2. Add the rest of the milk and heat until steaming but not boiling, stirring occasionally.

3. Remove from heat and stir in the vanilla.

4. Pour into mugs, then add marshmallows and a candy cane.

Yield: 2–3 servings

Winter Sweet Potato Soup

What you need:

- 2 large sweet potatoes
- 1 tablespoon unsalted butter
- 1 tablespoon flour
- 1 can (14 ounces) chicken or vegetable broth
- 1 tablespoon light brown sugar
- ¼ teas. ground ginger
- ⅛ teas. ground nutmeg
- Dash of ground cinnamon
- 1 cup milk
- Salt and pepper to taste

For baking potatoes: Preheat oven to 400° F. Pierce each potato several times with a fork. Place the sweet potatoes on a baking sheet lined with foil and bake for 45 minutes, or until tender.

For microwaving potatoes: Pierce each potato several times with a fork. Place on a microwave-safe plate and cook on high for 8 to 10 minutes or until tender, turning the potatoes once halfway through.

Directions

1. Bake or microwave sweet potatoes until soft and easily pierced with a fork.

2. Let potatoes cool (about 5 minutes), then peel away skin and cut into small pieces. The potatoes should be mushy. Set aside.

3. Add the butter and flour to a large pot and heat over medium heat, stirring constantly for several minutes.

4. Add the broth and brown sugar. Bring the mixture to a boil, then reduce heat to simmer.

5. Add the potatoes and spices, and cook for 5 minutes.

6. Carefully pour the soup into a blender in small batches. Puree the soup and put in a separate pot.

7. Add the milk to the puree and heat until warm.

8. Add salt and pepper to taste. Top with items like crushed pretzels, croutons, bacon bits, or cheese.

Yield: 4–6 servings

Accordion Potatoes

What you need:

- 6 medium potatoes (we recommend russet)
- 2 tablespoon olive oil
- Salt and pepper
- Your favorite spices (we recommend rosemary and garlic)

Directions

1. Preheat oven to 375° F.

2. Scrub each potato clean under cool water. Dry thoroughly.

3. Thinly slice the potatoes about $2/3$ of the way through.

4. Drizzle each potato with olive oil, then add salt, pepper, and spices to taste.

5. Bake for 45 minutes to 1 hour, or until potatoes are soft on the inside and crispy on the outside.

Yield: 6 servings

Christmas Pasta Bake

What you need:

- 1 package (1 pound) penne pasta
- 1 sweet onion, chopped
- 2 tablespoon olive oil
- 3 garlic cloves, minced
- 2 24-ounce jars marinara sauce
- ¾ cup chicken broth
- 1 med. red bell pepper, chopped
- Dash of salt
- 12 ounces fresh mozzarella slices
- ¾ cup fresh basil

Directions

1. Preheat oven to 350° F.

2. Cook the pasta according to the directions on the box. Drain and set aside.

3. Cook onion in olive oil in a large pot over medium-high heat for 6 to 8 minutes or until tender. Add garlic and cook for 1 minute more.

4. Stir in marinara sauce, chicken broth, red bell pepper, and salt.

5. Bring to a boil, then cover and simmer for 10 minutes.

6. Remove from heat and add cooked pasta.

7. Carefully transfer the pasta mixture to a greased 13 x 9 baking dish.

8. Top with cheese.

9. Bake for 20–25 minutes or until the cheese is golden. Garnish with basil.

Yield: 8 servings

Colorful Christmas Poke Cake

Directions

1. Prepare the two cake mixes according to the directions on the box in 9" round pans. Allow cakes to cool completely.

2. While cakes cool, pour the 1 cup of boiling water into one small bowl and pour the other cup into another bowl. Add the red gelatin package to the first bowl and the green gelatin package to the second bowl. Stir until the powder has dissolved.

3. Pierce the cakes all over, about 2/3 of the way down, with a fork. Pour the red mixture over one cake and the green mixture over the other.

4. Allow the cakes to set in the fridge for 3–4 hours.

5. When cakes have set, remove them from their pans. You can either make a double cake or two separate cakes. If making one cake, frost in between the two cakes and on top. If making two cakes, simply frost the tops.

6. Refrigerate for 45 minutes, then add sprinkles for decoration and serve.

Yield: 10–12 servings

What you need:

- 2 boxes of white cake mix
- 1 package (3 ounces) red gelatin
- 1 package (3 ounces) green gelatin
- 2 cups boiling water
- Whipped topping or your favorite frosting
- Sprinkles for decoration

Bear's Christmas Cut-Out Cookies

What you need:

<u>Cookies</u>
- 1 cup butter
- 2 cups granulated sugar
- 1 teas. vanilla
- 2 eggs
- 4 cups flour
- 2 teas. baking powder
- ½ teas. salt

<u>Frosting</u>
- 8 ounces cream cheese at room temperature
- 4 tablespoon (½ stick) unsalted butter at room temperature
- 1 pound powdered sugar
- 1 tablespoon vanilla extract
- Sprinkles or decorations of your choice

Directions

1. Combine cookie ingredients in a large mixing bowl. Beat on medium speed until smooth.

2. Chill dough in the fridge for 30 minutes, then roll out and cut using a bear-shaped cookie cutter.

3. Bake at 350° F for 8–10 minutes or till desired color.

4. While cookies cool, make frosting by beating cream cheese and butter in a large bowl until smooth. Slowly add powdered sugar, one cup at a time. Add vanilla extract.

5. Frost and decorate.

Yield: 2 dozen cookies

Kitchen Measurements

Standard		Metric conversion	
	8 Pinches = 1 Tablespoon		15 ml
	2 Tablespoons = 1/8 Cup		30 ml
	4 Tablespoons = 1/4 Cup		60 ml
	3 Teaspoons = 1 Tablespoon		15 ml
	5 Tablespoons + 1 Teaspoon = 1/3 Cup		75 ml
	8 Tablespoons = 1/2 Cup		120 ml
	16 Tablespoons = 1 Cup		240 ml
	2 Cups = 1 Pint		470 ml
	2 Pints = 1 Quart		.95 liter
	4 Cups = 1 Quart		.95 liter
	4 Quarts = 1 Gallon		3.8 liters